DWIGHT D. EISENHOWER

A Life from Beginning to End

Copyright © 2017 by Hourly History

Table of Contents

Introduction

"I like Ike" was more than a campaign slogan for Dwight D. Eisenhower's run for the presidency in 1952. The West Point graduate and World War II Supreme Commander in charge of the Normandy invasion was indeed likable; even Bernard Montgomery, the irascible British general who believed that he was the supremely qualified military leader who should have been named the Supreme Commander, called Eisenhower a nice chap, adding in, however, the remark that he was "no soldier." Whatever deficiencies Montgomery believed that Eisenhower displayed as a soldier, the Kansas-born American's contribution to the global conflict that established the United States as a world power had created a sufficiently impressive resume to provide him with a presidential gloss. He would serve as the nation's thirty-fourth president, but in his youth, no one saw the signs of greatness that would take him so far. Eisenhower was not one to boast of his abilities; he let his work do his boasting for him and that trait, combined with an awesome knack for getting things done, helped to turn the tide of war.

But how does the son of a Mennonite pacifist turn into a soldier? How does an average West Point student become so proficient that the hard-to-please George Marshall helped to further his career? How did the president with the military background become the seer who warned the country, in his last address to the nation before leaving office, to beware of the military-industrial complex?

Behind the genial exterior was a complicated man. The only reason he became a soldier was because he could receive a free college education if he went to West Point. As a soldier who never got the chance to go into combat during World War I, he feared that his career would languish. But throughout his life and career, opportunity was always waiting; sometimes it manifested itself during hard times, and even Lady Luck seemed to like Ike.

Chapter One

Calling Kansas Home

"Farming looks mighty easy when your plow is a pencil and you're a thousand miles from the corn field."

—Dwight D. Eisenhower

The third son of David and Ida Eisenhower, who entered the world on October 14, 1890, was born at home in Denison, Texas. The family's long-ago origins were in Germany and the original name, Eisenhauer, was changed to Eisenhower at some point during the journey that took them from Germany to Pennsylvania to finally

Kansas in the 1880s. The family was of farming stock, but David Eisenhower had gone to college to become an engineer rather than following the family's farming tradition. Ida Stover Eisenhower had gone to college as well, and she and her husband were married on the campus of Lane University in 1885. They moved to Hope, Kansas where David Eisenhower owned a store but when the economy went sour and the business failed, the family moved to Texas, living there from 1889 to 1892. Then they moved back to Kansas where David Eisenhower worked as a mechanic, first for the railroad and then with a creamery.

Dwight David Eisenhower spent his youth in the small farm town of Abilene, Kansas, one of the seven Eisenhower sons born to a poor family. He was originally named David Dwight after his father, but his mother switched the names because having two Davids in the family was too confusing. Even though his father wasn't a farmer, he worked in a creamery, one of the agricultural industries that depended upon farming. The nickname "Ike" was a family moniker bestowed upon all the boys, but only Dwight would continue to be called that into adulthood.

His mother, Ida Stover Eisenhower, a Mennonite, was a religious pacifist who opposed war and preferred peaceful solutions to violent ones. As a boy, Eisenhower had a notable temper; his mother's advice in response to a childhood incident would help provide him with the guidance he needed to control his anger. Older brothers Arthur and Edgar were going out to trick or treat on Halloween, but his parents didn't let Dwight join them. Their third son retaliated by venting his anger on an apple tree outside in the yard, not stopping until he'd bloodied his hand. His father sent the boy to bed, crying.

Mrs. Eisenhower went into his bedroom and sat in the rocking chair by his bed. She talked to him about anger and how it could come to control a person's actions if allowed to do so. She talked, and bandaged his hands, and gave him a good night kiss. The boy fell asleep but the lessons she taught him resonated. Eisenhower's technique for handling his emotions would later show self-discipline; on a piece of paper, he would write down the name of the person who had roused him to anger. Throughout his life, his temper would be a part of his personality, but his self-control made sure that it didn't rule him.

Eisenhower displayed no impressive academic prowess during his school years, although he did enjoy studying history. He preferred sports for his leisure activities and also enjoyed hunting and fishing. In 1909, after graduating from Abilene High School, Eisenhower worked for a year in the creamery, as well as working as a fireman, so that his brother would be able to attend college. That was part of a deal that he and older brother Edgar had made; Edgar had also agreed to work so that Dwight could go to college. But Edgar got a reprieve. In 1910, Eisenhower learned that all he had to do to get a free college education was to attend West

Point Military Academy. The graduate had no particular interest in becoming a soldier, but free college was a potent lure, enough to make the lackluster student study hard, pass the test, and enroll at the prestigious school.

Eisenhower's fondness for sports over academics followed him from Kansas and he lacked what the military instructors regarded as a sufficiently focused approach to his studies. Their prediction was that he had the potential to become a good officer, but no one saw the heights to which he would climb as a military leader. Although not academically inclined, he did, however, enjoy reading about military commanders of the past, that love of history having been nurtured years earlier by his mother. Eisenhower liked to play cards, play pranks, and, until he blew out his knee, play football for the school.

In 1915, Eisenhower graduated from West Point; his ranking was 61st out of a class of 164. His class would later distinguish itself as "the class the stars fell on" and with good reason: of those 164 graduates in 1915, 59 later became generals, the most of any class in West Point's history.

The new second lieutenant was sent to Fort Sam Houston in San Antonio, Texas, where he met another military man destined for fame: George S. Patton, Jr. For young officers serving what amounted to an apprenticeship, the years after World War I seemed interminable. They were ambitious and eager to advance, and that was the case for Eisenhower as well. But the lessons that he learned as a soldier in a peacetime army were building a foundation that would stand him in good stead when another world war loomed.

Chapter Two

Eisenhower, West Point Graduate

"We succeed only as we identify in life, or in war, or in anything else, a single overriding objective, and make all other considerations bend to that one objective."

—Dwight D. Eisenhower

George S. Patton, Jr. and Eisenhower soon found that they shared some innovative ideas to improve the army's fighting ability, but those ideas would bring controversy and, for Eisenhower, the risk of court martial.

Patton and controversy seemed to go hand-in-hand often, and the time would come when it would be up to Eisenhower to chasten his friend, but by that time, he would no longer be a second lieutenant.

There were no omens of his future at Fort Sam Houston and his military career looked bleak. In order to advance in the military, a young officer wanted to see combat. Eisenhower did not serve in France during World War I and he chafed at what he saw as inactivity; his war was spent training troops in Georgia, Kansas, Maryland and Pennsylvania. The military recognized his acumen at organization, which meant that his service was put to use as part of the mobilizing that took place on the home front. But finally, in November, 1918, he thought he was about to achieve his goal when he was ordered to go to Europe to lead a tank battalion. That military rite of passage was denied him when the armistice was signed on November 11.

Three years after graduating from West Point, the war was over and Eisenhower had no combat experience. But 1919 would provide yet another of the crucial building blocks in the making of a leader when Eisenhower, as part of the 1919

Transcontinental Motor Convoy, traveled with an Army convoy of 72 military vehicles on a mission. The convoy began at the White House and concluded two months later in San Francisco.

Army leaders realized that a network of roads crossing the country was needed for the defense of the nation. The goal was to establish the understanding that motor vehicles played an important role in the military and that these vehicles needed to be tested on the country's diverse landscapes. Decades later, Eisenhower would remember that trek across the country when he was planning a national highway system.

However, at the time, there was no indication that Eisenhower would ever be planning anything on a national scale. The following year, 1920, saw Eisenhower back at Fort Meade serving as the 305th Tank Brigade's second-in-command. He and the 304th Tank Brigade's commander, George S. Patton, Jr, renewed their friendship. He and Patton were focused on the army of the early twentieth century, and the two soldiers were impressed with the potential that tanks had to galvanize military engagements.

The two men were well aware of how the stagnation of trench warfare had contributed to the carnage of the global conflict that left Europe a graveyard. Europe had just emerged from the devastating conflagration of World War I, and its nations were struggling to acclimate to a new style of warfare that had disrupted the pattern of their lives. Tanks, Eisenhower and Patton believed, could make the difference in giving war an efficiency that would, ultimately, aid in victory. Patton was lucky enough to have a wider circle of contacts that included the Secretary of War, but no one was listening to two young men who thought tanks were the way of the future. When the 1920 National Defense Act abandoned the Tank Corps in favor of placing tanks in the infantry, Patton rejoined the cavalry.

Eisenhower was able to express his thoughts in writing with clarity and skill, a talent he had displayed at West Point when he finished writing his papers swiftly while his roommate needed several hours. The November 1920 issue of *Infantry Journal* examined the role that tanks had played in World War I. Eisenhower, the author of the role, acknowledged the flaws in the American Mark VIII tanks as well as the lighter Renaults built by the French. He was confident that the early versions of the tanks would be improved as the technology advanced. Eisenhower's vision of a tank that overcame these flaws would ultimately bear a resemblance to what would play a role in World War II, the M4 Sherman tank.

Eisenhower advocated the replacement of the divisional machine gun battalion, which did not have cross-country mobility although it was motorized, with a tank company. A company of fifteen fighting tanks, Eisenhower asserted, with half the number of vehicles and personnel that a machine gun battalion needed, would excel in firepower and maneuverability. Tanks could support infantry attacks better and longer, and they could carry more ammunition. Eisenhower encouraged military minds to look to the future. "The clumsy, awkward and snail-like progress of the old tanks must be forgotten, and in their place we must picture this speedy, reliable and efficient engine of destruction."

But traditional thought held that the purpose of all combat arms was to assist the infantry as it moved forward in battle. Even though there were some who perceived that tanks had the ability to clear a passage for soldiers to fight, and that artillery and tanks had their place in modern warfare, the Chief of Infantry, upon seeing the article, threatened to have Eisenhower court martialed if he continued to write material that ran counter to accepted infantry doctrine.

Perhaps the military minds of this era were simply locked in a transitional mindset between the style of warfare they had been taught and the daunting look of the future of war; they were as resistant to tanks as they were to airplanes, and Brigadier General Billy Mitchell had paid the price for his foresight in predicting that airpower would play a significant role in the future. Mitchell's career was over, but Eisenhower managed to avoid the peril of being an unwelcome seer. Fortunately, the passage of time would present tanks in a new light, and by 1925, technology was making a difference. In 1927, mechanization of the military was already established as part of military planning. While the episode did not benefit Eisenhower's career because of the obtuse leadership which could not advance its thinking, it did demonstrate his ability to recognize the need for change in military technology.

Chapter Three

Eisenhower Advances

"In preparing for battle I have always found that plans are useless, but planning is indispensable."

Dwight D. Eisenhower

No one could blame Eisenhower for despairing of his future in 1920 and 1921. In addition to his career woes, Eisenhower had suffered in his personal life. When he was transferred to Fort Sam Houston, Eisenhower met a woman he described as "a vivacious and attractive girl, smaller than average, saucy in the look about her face and in her whole attitude."

On Valentine's Day the following year, Eisenhower and Mary Geneva Doud were engaged when he gave her a miniature version of his class ring from West Point. "Mamie" was the daughter of a man who made such a fortune in the meat-packing industry that he was able to retire at the age of thirty-six. The family had servants and multiples homes, and Mamie enjoyed a comfortable life. To exchange that to be a military wife meant that her life would be vastly different from what she was used to. Still, she was in love, and her family approved of Eisenhower as a marital prospect.

The couple had originally planned a November wedding, but when the United States entered World War I, the engaged pair decided to move the date, given what they assumed was the likelihood that Eisenhower would see combat. The couple married at her parents' home in Denver on July 1. As a military wife, Mamie would move with her husband more than thirty times during their first thirty-five years of marriage. The year after their wedding, their son Doud Dwight, known as "Icky" was born.

In 1920, at the end of what had been a trying professional year for Eisenhower, the family was celebrating Christmas at Eisenhower's post in Camp Meade, Maryland. Eisenhower and his colleague George Patton had caught the attention of Brigadier General Fox Conner, who was impressed with their vision and who, unlike the other brass, was not leery of their stance on the role that tanks could play in war.

But then the Eisenhowers' son contracted scarlet fever and died in early January of the following year, a tragedy which his father recalled as "the greatest disappointment and disaster of my life." The death of his son led to a potential scandal in his military career when Eisenhower honestly informed the military that he had mistakenly received $250.67 in child support while Icky was staying with an aunt in Iowa. The Inspector General became involved in the investigation over the next couple of months, and there was the risk that Eisenhower would be discharged. Luckily, Brigadier General Conner intervened on Eisenhower's behalf, and the charges against him were dropped.

Nothing could replace the loss of their son, although the Eisenhowers would welcome a second son, John, in 1922. While the tragedy of family grief remained, his professional career was destined to improve when Eisenhower joined Brigadier General Fox Conner's staff in Panama.

Serving with Conner meant that Eisenhower was working in the Panama Canal Zone under an officer who perceived the value of his views on infantry warfare. Thanks to Conner, Eisenhower was appointed in 1926 as a student at the Command and General Staff College at Fort Leavenworth, which he considered as "a year which should be one of the most enjoyable, and in many ways the finest of an officer's peacetime service." Graduating first out of 245 officers, Eisenhower immediately benefitted from the move when he was named as an aide to General John J. Pershing, who had been the commander of American troops during World War I.

Under Pershing, who was the chairman of the American Battle Monuments Commission (ABMC), Eisenhower spent a year in France, where, in addition to writing a guidebook to the battlefields of World War I, he became acquainted with the people of France, their landscape and their culture, and transportation systems. That knowledge was yet another of the pieces that would come into play years later when he was serving in Europe as the Supreme Allied Commander.

His next assignment would prove to be both challenging and fortuitous when he joined Army Chief of Staff General Douglas MacArthur and served with him for seven years. Subordinate to MacArthur, Eisenhower did not always agree with him and that separation of thought manifested itself during the conflict with the Bonus Marchers.

World War I veterans had been rewarded with certificates that would be redeemable in 1945 for $1,000 each. But between the end of World War I and that year, the Great Depression plunged the world into financial ruin. The veterans, many of whom were out of work at a time when the employment rate for the nation was twenty-five percent, couldn't wait until 1945; they needed the money immediately. They asked Congress to redeem their certificates early. Calling themselves the Bonus Expeditionary Force, the veterans headed for Washington D.C. By the time they arrived, they numbered 15,000. Because many of them traveled with wives and families, the community was even larger.

President Herbert Hoover, his administration mired in the country's economic nightmare, refused to meet the Bonus Marchers. A congressional delegation did meet with them and deliberated in legislative session over whether they should redeem the certificates. During the deliberations, the Bonus Army was living in a makeshift shantytown across the Potomac River. The Senate voted against redeeming the certificates early, and many of the veterans left the capital. Most, but not all; several thousand, many who had nowhere to go, stayed. Fearing a possible threat, the Washington police began to clear the Bonus Army out of their shantytown.

Then, President Hoover sent the army in under the direction of MacArthur, with Major George Patton leading the cavalry and Major Eisenhower serving as the Army's liaison to the D.C. police. As the soldiers and six tanks prepared to move on the Marchers, civilian onlookers, sympathetic to the plight of the veterans, were horrified when the troops, bayonets fixed, charged the crowd. The veterans crossed the river, and President Hoover told the army to halt, but

MacArthur, ignoring the Commander-in-Chief's order, led the infantry to the veteran's main camp. Two babies were killed, the neighboring hospitals were filled with casualties, the Bonus Army scattered, and MacArthur gave orders that the shantytown was to be burned. Writing of what he had witnessed, Eisenhower reveals his emotions, noting that "the whole scene was pitiful. The veterans were ragged, ill-fed, and felt themselves badly abused. To suddenly see the whole encampment going up in flames just added to the pity."

In 1935, MacArthur was named military advisor to the Philippines and

Eisenhower went with him. Their assignment was to train the Filipino Army. The two men were diametrical opposites, and Eisenhower described the difference between them succinctly when he said, years later, "I studied dramatics under him for five years in Washington and four years in the Philippines." One of MacArthur's ideas for showing how the army had bonded was to organize a parade for the soldiers. The Philippines' president objected because of the cost and the time involved in the parade. MacArthur then blamed Eisenhower for the parade, an embarrassment that Eisenhower did not forget. Once again, however, the lessons he learned in working with an egotistical superior officer would be of good use when he was the officer in charge of handling another brilliant egoist, General Bernard Montgomery.

Chapter Four

Eisenhower in Charge

"Okay, let's go."

—Dwight D. Eisenhower

Well into his career by this time, Eisenhower had not distinguished himself in battle but he had established himself as a superbly capable administrator. Both General Pershing and General MacArthur viewed him as the most promising officer they had worked with. In 1939, Eisenhower left the Philippines and returned to the United States, where he was named Chief of Staff of the

Third Army. The year 1939 saw war break out in Europe but the United States, intent on staying out of the conflict, remained on the sidelines, although prescient minds knew that isolation could not last.

Eisenhower showed his skill in overseeing the training of 420,000 soldiers in Louisiana. His work was noticed and he was promoted to the rank of brigadier general. Days after the United States declared war on Japan following the attack on Pearl Harbor, Eisenhower found himself in the nation's capital working on the war plans with Army Chief of Staff George C. Marshall, a man not given to praise. But Marshall appreciated the skills and strategic insights of Eisenhower, who had been recommended to the stern leader by General Pershing. Defeating the Nazi menace would require more than just battlefield strategy; it required planning and preparation and it was in these areas that Eisenhower excelled.

Eisenhower also excelled at handling prima donnas in uniform and standing firm without surrendering his own authority or grasp of the ultimate goals. He inspired respect in those who worked for him, and he was adept at choosing subordinates whose qualities made them perform well. The cast of characters involved in the saving of the Free World did not always put their cause ahead of their egos. Eisenhower was used to that and knew how to handle it.

The days when he was a junior officer in hot water for promoting modern innovations in warfare were well behind him, but Eisenhower had the advantage of knowing how to learn and retaining the lessons. His value in the war strategy made him an integral player in the preparations. He was in command of the Allies for Operation Torch, the invasion of North Africa in 1942. He followed that with the direction of the invasions of Italy and Sicily.

The Allies and Axis powers alike both knew that it was a matter of time until the armies of the America, Britain, and Canada returned to Europe, but the Germans were the masters of the territory they had won at the start of the war. Russia's leader Joseph Stalin wanted a second front but the magnitude of a landing, although in the planning stages as early as the British retreat from Dunkirk, would be a massive venture. Meeting in Casablanca, the Allied representatives, including President Franklin Roosevelt, Prime Minister

Winston Churchill, and French General Henri Giraud, agreed that the only terms that would be offered to the Germans would be unconditional surrender.

The British were hesitant about an invasion into Western Europe, which was controlled by the Nazis, but the Allies convinced—or overruled—Winston Churchill and June was designated as the month when the Allies would begin the final stage of the war.

Eisenhower had risen from a lieutenant colonel before the war to a four-star general as the war progressed. His fears during World War I that he would fail to be promoted due to a lack of combat experience were swiftly dispelled as the military's need for his skills and abilities accelerated his progress. In January 1944, Eisenhower was named Supreme Allied Commander, and the invasion of Normandy, code named Operation Overlord, was gearing up for implementation.

Moving the largest invasion force—7,000 ships and landing craft, 195,000 naval personnel, 133,000 troops—in the history of the world was no small matter. Not only did Eisenhower have to oversee the huge logistical challenge of the undertaking, a task which was under his direct control, but he had to deal with the weather, which played no favorites. By the time June arrived, Eisenhower had a mere four days of potentially good weather for the invasion. Then, on June 4, the English Channel saw inclement weather and Eisenhower considered postponing the invasion because conditions were supposed to get worse over the coming two weeks. The Germans were confident that poor weather would ruin the chances of an invasion. Eisenhower had to decide. "I don't like it," he told his generals, "but we have to go."

On June 5, at 9:45 at night, the weather report was promising. Eisenhower made the decision to proceed with the invasion, telling his staff, "Okay, let's go." The next day, each soldier, sailor, and airman who was part of Operation Overlord received a statement written by Eisenhower:

Soldiers, Sailors and Airmen of the Allied Expeditionary Forces:

You are about to embark upon the Great Crusade, toward which we have striven these many months. . . . The hopes and prayers of liberty-loving people everywhere march with you. In company with our brave Allies and brothers-in-arms on other Fronts you will bring about the destruction of the German war machine, the elimination of Nazi tyranny over oppressed peoples of Europe, and security for ourselves in a free world.

Your task will not be an easy one. Your enemy is well trained, well equipped and battle-hardened. He will fight savagely.

But this is the year 1944 . . . The tide has turned . . . We will accept nothing less than full victory."

It was a stirring message. What was not known at the time was that, in

Eisenhower's pocket, was another message, one to be delivered if the invasion failed. Eisenhower had written, "The troops, the air and the Navy did all that bravery and devotion to duty could do. If any blame or fault attaches to the attempt it is mine alone." He had underlined the words "mine alone."

Waiting for word of the invasion, President Roosevelt was informed by telephone at 3:00 am on June 6 that the invasion had begun. That night, Americans learned of the invasion of Normandy. Eisenhower did not need to deliver the second statement.

On June 8, Eisenhower reported that the invasion was a success. By the end of the month, more than 850,000 men, with 570,000 tons of supplies and 148,000 vehicles were on the shores of Normandy Beach. The invasion was costly, and many young men lost their lives, but the Allies were now on their way to conquering the Nazis who had cast such a dark, malignant shadow over Europe for so long. Once again, the strategic and masterful planning of Eisenhower was a success.

Chapter Five

The Post-War Eisenhower

"Though force can protect in emergency, only justice, fairness, consideration and co-operation can finally lead men to the dawn of eternal peace."

—Dwight D. Eisenhower

On May 7, 1945, the Germans surrendered; Japan followed suit on September 2, persuaded by the most destructive force the world had ever witnessed, the dropping of the atomic bomb over Hiroshima and Nagasaki.

Eisenhower knew about the existence of the bomb but was opposed to using it because of his belief that it would tarnish the American victory. He wrote, "First, the Japanese were ready to surrender and it wasn't necessary to hit them with that awful thing. Second, I hated to see our country be the first to use such a weapon." Yet, it was not his decision to make.

As far as the United States was concerned, it was America that had won the war and that victory came in no small part because of the efforts of Dwight D. Eisenhower. The world was equally willing to acknowledge the heroism of the Supreme Allied

Commander and Eisenhower was feted in parades in his own nation's capital as well as in London, Paris, and Moscow.

Victory was complicated, and Eisenhower was at the center of some decisions which aroused controversy. Now that the Nazis were defeated, the expedience of the war-time alliance with Russia was called into question. But Eisenhower was a soldier, not a philosopher or a politician and he had orders. He permitted the Russian Army to liberate Berlin at the war's end. Acquiescing to the stipulation of the Yalta Conference which required all of the Soviet Union's citizens who were in the U.S. occupied zone to be returned to their homeland, Eisenhower felt that he did not have the authority to allow the political opposition to remain, even though the dissidents had no desire to go back to the fate that awaited them under Stalin. When George Patton, serving as Bavaria's military governor, violated the order about allowing ex-Nazis to serve in government positions, Eisenhower relieved him of his position. Eisenhower was following the orders as he understood them and those orders did not allow him to make decisions based on his own preferences.

Eisenhower was the military governor of the U.S. Occupation Zone in Germany; the other zones were under the control of Great Britain, France, and the Soviet Union. Some of Eisenhower's rulings were directly related to the role that the Germans had taken in the war. To strengthen the case against the Nazis in the Nuremberg Trials, Eisenhower sent camera crews to document the horrible acts that had taken place in the concentration camps. Although he had German prisoners of war reclassified as Disarmed Enemy Forces who were not subject to the rules of the Geneva Convention, he showed compassion for the people of

Germany, bringing in 400,000 tons of food, along with medical equipment, to ease the suffering caused by food shortages and the number of refugees in need.

With the end of the war, Eisenhower went back to the United States, where he was made the Army's Chief of Staff. Just as he had applied his administrative prowess to the preparation of the Normandy invasion, he was now working to demobilize the millions of soldiers who were returning from the front.

Still, the Cold War was underway, and Eisenhower was tasked with adapting the military for a new field of battle in a conflict which was fought indirectly, for ideology as well as conquest, as Soviet leaders sought to expand their influence in other parts of the world. Initially, Eisenhower had been confident that the Russians had peaceful intentions and that the post-war world could work together. He was a supporter of the newly created United Nations and thought it could be instrumental in overseeing the nuclear element which was transforming the nature of war. President Truman was less sanguine about Soviet intentions, and by 1947, as international tensions escalated, Eisenhower came to agree with Truman that Soviet expansion posed a genuine threat to national and international security, and he focused on developing a containment policy.

Despite his long-lasting wishes for peace, it was Eisenhower who would later coin the phrase "the domino theory" to explain the vulnerable connections between nations which could lead to Soviet domination.

In 1948, *Crusade in Europe*, Eisenhower's memoir, was published to critical and financial success. That same year, he was named the president of Columbia University. During this time, he led a group which considered the effects, both political and military, of the American Marshall Plan which was designed to bring aid to war-ravaged Europe. As a soldier by training rather than an academic, Eisenhower was not only an administrator but also in charge of the university's educational direction. His education was ongoing as he became involved in the Council on Foreign Relations, a position which provided him with an introduction to economics. This would be useful to him when he embarked upon a political career, but Eisenhower was not, at this time, intent upon the presidency. His goal, instead, was to promote American democracy through education.

Eisenhower was by no means isolated in an ivory tower, and he was asked to serve as an advisor to Truman's Secretary of Defense who was seeking his counsel on the unification of the military. Shortly after that, he began to offer his advice on an informal basis to the Joint Chiefs of Staff as they endeavored to steer the nation through the threat of nuclear weapons, which soon were no longer solely the possession of the United States.

His creation of the American Assembly, which was part of his plan to promote American democracy, had been transformed from a concept to an institution, and he began to travel around the country to solicit financial support. To the faculty and staff of Columbia University, who were struggling with the uncertainty of knowing how to deal with a president who was not an academic, Eisenhower's efforts looked as though he was buttressing his own career at the expense of Columbia. It's true that he was building a network of contacts through his travels, one which would prove effective when he was a candidate for president not of the university but of the nation, but Eisenhower wasn't working with a secret agenda.

The presidency of Columbia was a bridge for the soldier to transfer from the military to the civilian realm of influence. But outside influences were also at play when he submitted his resignation in 1950 in order to become the commander of the North Atlantic Treaty Organization with operational command of the forces.

Columbia's trustees refused to accept his resignation, and when he retired from active military service in 1952, he returned. He held this position until January 20, 1953, when he became the President of the United States.

Chapter Six

From Commander to Candidate

"Life-long professional soldiers, in the absence of some obvious and overriding reason, [should] abstain from seeking high political office."

—Dwight D. Eisenhower

The suggestion that after the war, Eisenhower might want to consider running for office had been broached as early as 1943. However, Eisenhower was firm: a general had no place in politics and he dismissed the suggestion. As the interest in seeing Eisenhower as a political candidate continued to mount, Eisenhower scoffed at the idea that he had interest in any political office, whether it was a "political post from dogcatcher to Grand High Supreme King of the Universe." Speaking seriously, he felt that he could not be effective in his job as the Army Chief of Staff if people felt that he had political aspirations. When he attended the Potsdam Conference, President Truman had offered to help Eisenhower if he wished to run for president in 1948; in 1947, Truman said that if Eisenhower ran, Truman was willing to serve as his running mate on the Democratic ticket.

Douglas MacArthur was rumored to be the Republican's choice.

Upon learning that New Hampshire planned to elect delegates to support his candidacy at the Republican National Convention, Eisenhower's response was that he could not accept a nomination to high political office. Not only had Eisenhower never run for office, but he had never even voted and had no party affiliation.

President Truman had been re-elected in the 1948 election, but unpopularity over his firing of General MacArthur and the lack of progress in the war in Korea gave the

Republicans confidence at their chances of winning the White House in 1952. An "Eisenhower for President" movement began to gain traction in the Republican Party, even though Senator Robert Taft was regarded as the Party's frontrunner. Officially, Eisenhower said that his responsibilities as the NATO commander in Europe were his chief interest, but when Senator Henry Cabot Lodge visited him at NATO headquarters in Paris, Eisenhower was less reluctant when asked to be the standard-bearer for the Republican Party. In January 1952, Eisenhower announced that he was a Republican and that he was willing to serve the American people once again, this time as president.

Taft wasn't willing to concede to the popular general, however, and he had the lead in delegates. Behind-the-scenes maneuvering at the convention managed to win Eisenhower the nomination on the first ballot. Richard Nixon, senator from California, won the vice-presidential nomination, thanks in part to his efforts to bring in votes for Eisenhower from California delegates. He had the edge over his democratic opponent, Governor Adlai Stevenson, who was certainly qualified, as a lawyer, an assistant to the Secretary of the Navy during the war, and a successful governor.

But Ike had the war victory on his resume. He had a cheerful demeanor and a forthright, reassuring speaking style. He visited forty-five of the nation's forty-eight states to campaign. He was part of a new innovation, television commercials, which brought political campaigning via a new medium. Americans were ready for a change and were eager to respond to Eisenhower's charm.

Corruption in the Truman administration had inspired Eisenhower to promise that this own presidency would be as clean as a hound's tooth, but that claim appeared baseless when Richard Nixon was accused of using campaign funds for his own use. To refute the accusations, Nixon went on the air to deliver a speech, forever known as the "Checkers Speech," in which he asserted his innocence, and said that the only gift he had accepted was a dog, named Checkers, that he would not give up because the dog was his daughters' pet. The speech was convincing, and Nixon remained the vice presidential candidate.

Harry Truman had moved far away from his previous stance of support for

Eisenhower. He went on his own campaign to criticize Eisenhower for his Wall Street ties and for failing to be his own person but instead serving as a Republican puppet.

Eisenhower promised that if he became president, he would go to Korea and for a nation that was tired of a war that appeared to be going nowhere, the promise was powerful. Eisenhower won fifty-five percent of the popular vote, not only winning Republican states but also doing well in the South, winning traditionally Democratic states. It was significant that the voters who chose Eisenhower for president were voting not for the party, but for the man; other Republican candidates did not fare so well, and there was no landslide mandate bringing in a GOP majority. Eisenhower, meeting with advisors before his inauguration, discussed the major issues he foresaw in his presidency. His goals in his first term were to balance the budget, end the war in Korea, promote nuclear deterrence, and end price and wage controls. Eisenhower also explained his policy toward Russia. The government recognized that the Soviet quest for domination in the world would be a focal point for the Eisenhower and successive presidential administrations.

It was probably no surprise that the president who, as a general, had played a vital role in what may be regarded as the preeminent international episode of the twentieth century, focused on foreign policy in his inaugural address. Before delivering the address, Eisenhower took the oath of office using two Bibles. The first Bible had been used by the nation's first president, George Washington, at his first inauguration. The other Bible was the one that Ida Eisenhower, who died in 1946, had given to her son when he graduated from West Point. Although she felt that warfare was, as she had put it, wicked, she honored her son's achievement with a gift that fulfilled her beliefs and her hopes for him.

Chapter Seven

President Eisenhower

"The overwhelming majority of southerners, Negro and white, stand firmly behind your resolute action to restore law and order in Little Rock."

—Martin Luther King

Just as the Eisenhower years in America are regarded as a time of peace and stability between the drama of the 1940s war years and the upheaval of the 1960s, the President himself believed in a middle-of-the-road stance in his programs. Some conservative members of his party sought to eliminate the New Deal and Fair Deal programs of his predecessors but Eisenhower's "Modern Republicanism" did not turn its back on assisting the elderly and the unemployed who needed help. Ultra-conservative Republicans were not happy when Eisenhower not only continued Social Security but expanded it as he created a new Cabinet post, the Department of Health, Education and Welfare. His intention, he said, was to take the United States on a path of moderation "between the unfettered power of concentrated wealth . . . and the unbridled power of statism or partisan interests."

That promise indicated that there were undercurrents rising to the surface in American society. The bland reputation of the Eisenhower years is erroneous because social causes were beginning to stir the public. Civil rights was one area of dramatic change. The implementation of President Truman's intent to integrate the American military had been slow-going, but in his first State of the Union address, Eisenhower promised that he would use whatever authority he had as president to end segregation in the federal government and the Armed Forces. He met the expected resistance by controlling military spending to make his point that there was no justification for discrimination. His Secretary of the Navy felt that the customs that were in practice in particular parts of the nation (i.e., segregation and Jim Crow practices which separated the races and kept African-American citizens in a state of subjugation) should be observed and not ignored by the Navy, but Eisenhower's response was that "We have not taken and we shall not take a single backward step. There must be no second-class citizens in this country."

The civil rights issues reached beyond the military; in 1954, *Brown v. Board of Education of Topeka*, a Supreme

Court ruling, made racial segregation in the nation's public schools unconstitutional. Racism was not a subject upon which Eisenhower wanted to become deeply involved, and he was not sympathetic to the Supreme Court decision, but during his second term, he would be obliged to uphold the ruling by sending federal troops to Arkansas when Governor Orval Faubus tried to prevent African-American students from desegregating Little Rock's Central High School.

Eisenhower was aware that the rest of the world was avidly watching as the United States, which regarded itself as the beacon of light for democracy and freedom, came to recognize the double standard that allowed two races to operate on such opposite standards of equality.

The Communist regime in the Soviet Union chastised Americans for hypocrisy in its civil rights dealings. Eisenhower was well aware of the Soviet perspective, and he was vocal in his opposition to communism. Yet, that didn't make him an ally of Wisconsin's senator Joseph McCarthy, who had asserted in 1950 that the federal government was riddled with communist spies and sympathizers. McCarthy had been vociferous in his attacks on President Truman but having a Republican President didn't bring the attacks to an end, even though McCarthy's high-profile campaign had failed to expose traitors. Eisenhower, although he disagreed with McCarthy's methods, feared that if he directly confronted the anti-communist campaigner, the office of the presidency would be demeaned. Or, as Eisenhower put it, "I just won't get into a pissing contest with that skunk."

In 1954, McCarthy upped the stakes when he brought his charges that the Army was infiltrated by communists to a television audience, holding hearings before an America in which fifty-six percent of the homes had television. But it was television, as much as the president, that was McCarthy's undoing, as the public saw McCarthy not as the champion of the American way of life, but as a bully who made charges against people that could not be substantiated. In 1954, the Senate voted to censure McCarthy, bringing to an end his corrosive role in American politics.

Originally, Eisenhower had indicated that he would only want to serve a single term and when, in September of 1955, while he was on vacation, the President, a long-time heavy smoker, suffered a major heart attack, it seemed that a single term would be all he could do. Eisenhower was frank in disclosures about his health, and the press was kept informed of Eisenhower's progress during his six weeks recovery. The Vice President, Secretary of State Dulles, and White House Chief of Staff Sherman Adams took over the administrative duties of the government during this time and were in communication with the president. The doctor stated that Eisenhower's health was sufficiently improved to allow him to run for a second term. On February 29, 1956, Eisenhower, who had returned to a full schedule of activities, announced his plans to seek a second term.

That full schedule included the Federal-Aid Highway Act of 1956, which Eisenhower signed into law on June 29. The purpose of creating a 41,000-mile network of highways was to promote safe and fast transcontinental travel by eliminating traffic congestion, unsafe roadways, and routes that were inefficient. However, because it was the time of the Cold War when the threat of nuclear attack was a fear constantly in the minds of Americans, the network of highways also promised evacuation routes that would operate efficiently.

Eisenhower's first term had been a productive one, and his popularity indicated that he'd win re-election in the 1956 election. But, because of his heart attack, the vice presidential candidate was even more important. Nixon's experience was established, yet, there were other concerns, and Eisenhower tried to get the vice president to decline the nomination in order to establish himself for a presidential bid on his own in 1960, but Nixon wasn't going for it. The Eisenhower-Nixon ticket won in a landslide, carrying forty-one states. Once again, the people who voted for the popular president did not demonstrate equal enthusiasm for his party, and the Democrats still had control of Congress.

Chapter Eight

The Last Chapter

"Every gun that is made, every warship launched, every rocket fired signifies, in the final sense, a theft from those who hunger and are not fed, those who are cold and not clothed. This world in arms is not spending money alone. It is spending the sweat of its laborers, the genius of its scientists, the hopes of its children. This is not a way of life at all in any true sense.

Under the cloud of threatening war, it is humanity hanging from a cross of iron."

—Dwight D. Eisenhower

Eisenhower tried to strike a balance between the menace presented by Soviet aggression and his own Republican Party's resistance to a peaceful balance between the two superpowers. During his first term as president, Eisenhower had delivered what was known as his Chance for Peace speech, in which he promoted peaceful uses of nuclear materials in order to control the nuclear arms race. But the Soviets weren't interested in his proposals to have both nations move away from nuclear expansion in favor of the program that he called Atoms for Peace.

Eisenhower's perception of the Soviet domination in other parts of the world, particularly Southeast Asia and Central America, compared their ambitions to a series of dominoes; if the Soviets won in Vietnam, then, Eisenhower said, neighboring countries would fall, one by one.

This theory would dominate American politics for years ahead, and it would come particularly close to home near the end of Eisenhower's second term, as he supported a plan to invade Cuba in order to overthrow Fidel Castro, who had seized power and had the support of the Soviet Union. The disaster that would become famous as the Bay of Pigs invasion turned out to be a political crisis for his successor, the newly elected and untested President John F. Kennedy.

The Cold War was not only being fought across the continents. The Soviets were ahead of the United States in the ensuing Space Race, and in 1957, the word Sputnik made Americans fearful that the Russians were superior to them in technology, and the heavens were in danger of becoming Soviet territory. Eisenhower responded to the launch of Sputnik by promoting a campaign to upgrade the nation's ability to explore space, but he also sought to improve science education in the schools. The creation of the National Aeronautics and Space Administration (NASA) in 1958 proved that the Eisenhower administration did not intend to let the United States fall behind in this newest competition between enemies.

The assistance that Eisenhower's government, early in his first term, had provided in French Indochina to help against the Communists, increased during his second term; Eisenhower's concept of the domino theory meant that Vietnam could not be permitted to be taken over by a communist regime.

Negotiations between the two rivals were ongoing, but so were the plots against each other. The Soviet Union's Nikita Khrushchev had visited the United States in 1959, and President Eisenhower was scheduled to visit the Soviet Union in 1960. But on May 1, a U-2 spy plane piloted by Francis Gary Powers was shot down. The plane had been flying in Russian airspace to take photographs in advance of an upcoming summit. The United States did not want to admit to spying on its enemy, and Khrushchev had thought that the spy flights had come to an end, but the downing of the U-2 disproved America's claims of innocence.

The United States was quick with an explanation; instead of admitting that the plane had been spying on the Soviets, the report was that a weather plane had been lost. Because the Soviets didn't mention Powers, the assumption was that he had been killed when the plane went down. On May 5, Khrushchev countered that the plane, which had been spying and not reporting on the weather, had been shot down and the pilot captured. Powers was put on trial and three months later, convicted of espionage. The U-2 was displayed fully intact and not destroyed as the Americans had claimed. Following this, the summit, which was the intended subject of the photographs, did not take place. Eisenhower's hopes for an easing of tensions between the Soviet Union and the United States were dashed, and the Americans came out of the episode with national prestige damaged. Powers would not be released from his imprisonment during Eisenhower's presidency; he was exchanged for a Soviet intelligence officer and returned to the United States in 1962.

The Soviet Union was not the only region of unrest. The Middle East entered the spotlight under Eisenhower's term when the President forced Great Britain, France, and Israel to end their invasion of Egypt after Gamal Abdel Nasser nationalized the Suez Canal. The Eisenhower Doctrine said that the United States was prepared to use armed force in order to counter aggression from any country that was controlled by international communism. Eisenhower provided economic support to Jordan, and sent Marines and soldiers to Lebanon, but division over Israel, oil, and Zionism kept tensions high in the region, and the legacy would dominate American foreign policy for generations to come.

The 1960 election passed the torch to a new generation; Senator John F. Kennedy narrowly defeated Vice-President Richard Nixon in the presidential race. Eisenhower was not happy at the prospect of leaving the White House to his successor, the Democrat John F. Kennedy, admitting to his friends during the campaign that "I will do almost anything to avoid turning my chair and country over to Kennedy." Yet, his wishes were in vain, and the young Massachusetts senator took the oath of office in 1961 as a new decade would see the

United States embark upon a time of bold new frontiers and heart-wrenching tragedies.

Before Eisenhower left the White House, he left the country with a word of warning not only about the dangers of the Cold War but about the military-industrial complex and the threat of excessive government spending. He supported the maintenance of a strong military but worried that excessive military spending could endanger the country's hopes of peace and continued prosperity.

It was time for Dwight and Mamie Eisenhower to leave Washington D.C.

and return to their farm in Gettysburg, Pennsylvania. The working farm had been a favorite place even while he was in office, and it was not unknown for Eisenhower to invite international figures to come to Camp David and then for them to visit his farm. He enjoyed taking them on a tour of the grounds to see his herd of Angus cattle, and then returning to the farmhouse to sit on the porch, where the casual atmosphere gave him the opportunity to get to know the person better.

Gettysburg was also a favorite place for his wife. Mamie had been a very effective First Lady, and while she brought the precision of military life to White House routines, she also brought her own warmth. She endeared herself to Americans, who appreciated her celebrated fondness for the color pink, for her hair style, and for her candid affection for her husband. When their new bed arrived in the White House, Mamie said, "Now I can reach over and pat Ike on his old bald head any time I want to!"

After a lifetime of service in which their duty came first, the Eisenhowers were finally free to pursue their own personal pleasures. They enjoyed traveling in their retirement and Eisenhower was in reasonably good health for most of that time, able to travel abroad and also to receive visitors at home. Eisenhower remained an important political figure, supporting Republican candidates and speaking at the 1964 Republican Convention.

On March 28, 1969, Eisenhower died of congestive heart failure. His body lay in state in the rotunda of the Capitol. A funeral train, the last time a train would be included in an American president's funeral, took him back to Abilene, Kansas, where he was interred in the standard $80 soldier's casket on the grounds of his presidential library. He had been a soldier and a president, but he was buried as a general, wearing his green jacket and his medals. His young son, "Icky," who died in 1921 was buried beside him. Mamie Eisenhower, who died in 1979, was also buried at his side.

Richard Nixon, Eisenhower's vice president and a president in his own right, delivered the eulogy for his former boss and in his address, he touched on the central characteristic of Eisenhower's nature. "In the political world, strong passions are the norm and all too often these turn toward personal vindictiveness. People often disagreed with Dwight

Eisenhower, but almost nobody ever hated him. And this, I think, was because he, himself, was a man who did not know how to hate."

Conclusion

It takes time for a president to be accurately assessed, and in 1962, historians ranked Eisenhower twenty-second among his fellow presidents. As time went on, his reputation and standing improved, and when measured against the presidents who had held office in the last seventy-five years, he was surpassed only by Franklin D. Roosevelt and Harry S. Truman.

As his presidential papers became available in the 1970s, there was much more to Ike than golf, fishing, and bridge, three of his favorite leisure time activities. Eisenhower was shown to be a president very much involved in the decision-making process, whether meeting with his Cabinet or with the National Security Council.

Despite the tensions of the Cold War, Eisenhower was able to pursue a policy of peace that kept the nation safe. The nation prospered economically, helped by the construction of the Interstate Highway System that modernized America's travel network to meet the challenges of a mobile population. Confident in the nation's military, he didn't overreact with spending hikes after the Soviet space victory with Sputnik. He could have done more to promote civil rights; he could have been more proactive in challenging Joseph McCarthy; he could have resisted the quicksand of Vietnam that would pull the nation into a long and unpopular war. His record is not without its mistakes and misjudgments. But when he left the White House in 1961, he left a country that was enjoying peace and prosperity. There was no way of knowing that Vietnam would turn into a national tragedy or that the even keel of the Eisenhower 1950s would erupt into a generation that challenged the blandness of the past and forced a complacent country to confront what it had unknowingly ignored for so long.

One permanent legacy of the Eisenhower presidency is enjoyed by all of his successors although they may give little thought to its name. The presidential retreat known as Camp David had been called Shangri-La by Franklin Roosevelt, who made use of the secluded hideaway as a place where he could find refuge from Washington D.C. without being isolated from his duties. When Eisenhower first became president, he thought that having a presidential getaway was unnecessary and considered getting rid of it. But as he fell under the spell of the retreat, he put his own mark on it, adding picnic tables and a golf course. And a name.

When presidents get away from the gridlock of Washington D.C., Camp David is their sanctuary. It was named Camp David after Eisenhower's grandson, David Eisenhower, who was a child at the time. Eisenhower loved his family, and so it was that Shangri-La was christened.

Eisenhower was a better president than anyone expected him to be, just as he was a better general than his early military history indicated he would become. He didn't seek the spotlight, and he was willing to shoulder the blame and share the credit. The Eisenhower years are remembered fondly by those who lived during that time, and for those who remember the president, they would agree that it was very easy to like Ike.

Made in the USA
Columbia, SC
26 September 2023